HOW TO IMPROVE YOUR
BASKETBALL

CONSULTANTS

Dr. Forrest C. "Phog" Allen

Harold E. "Bud" Foster

Edward S. "Eddie" Hickey

REPRESENTING

The National Basketball Coaches' Association of the United States

PUBLISHED BY

THE ATHLETIC INSTITUTE
Merchandise Mart — Room 805
Chicago 54, Ill.

A non-profit organization devoted to the advancement of athletics, physical education and recreation.

Foreword

"How To Improve Your Basketball" is but one item in a comprehensive list of sports instruction aids made available on a non-profit basis by The Athletic Institute. The photographic material in this book has been reproduced in total from The Athletic Institute's sound, color slidefilm, "Basketball." This book and the slidefilm are parts of a program designed to bring the many benefits of athletics, physical education and recreation to everyone.

The Athletic Institute is a non-profit organization devoted to the advancement of athletics, physical education and recreation. It functions on the premise that athletics and recreation bring benefits of inestimable value to the individual and to the community.

The nature and scope of the many Institute programs are determined by an advisory committee of selected persons noted for their outstanding knowledge, experience and ability in the fields of athletics, physical education and recreation.

It is their hope, and the hope of the Institute, that through this book, the reader will become a better basketball player, skilled in the fundamentals of this fine sport. Knowledge, and the practice necessary to mold knowledge into actual ability, are the keys to real enjoyment of playing basketball.

TABLE OF CONTENTS

Basketball Court Diagram	Page 4
UNIT One — The Game	Page 5
UNIT Two — Ball Handling	Page 15
— Receiving	Page 18
UNIT Three — Passing	Page 24
— Chest	Page 25
— Over-the-Shoulder	Page 27
— Underhand	Page 30
UNIT Four — Dribbling	Page 35
UNIT Five — Pivoting	Page 43
UNIT Six — Shooting	Page 51
— Push Shots	Page 52
— Lay-Ups	Page 55
— Free Throws	Page 60
UNIT Seven — Defense	Page 63
History of the Game	Page 73
Basic Basketball Rules	Page 75
Some Common Basketball Terms	Page 78
Bibliography	Page 80

THE BASKETBALL COURT

UNIT ONE

IMPROVE YOUR

GAME

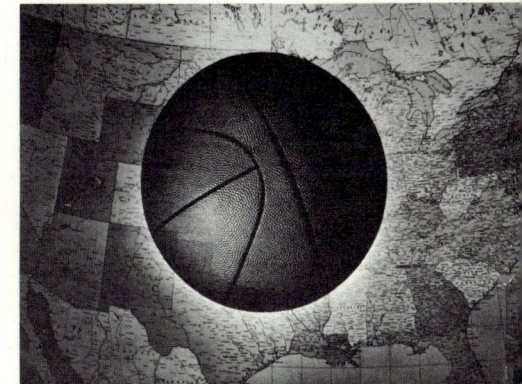

Basketball is one of the few major sports that originated entirely in the United States. Other games, as we know them today, evolved from sports of other lands. But basketball is as American as the National anthem.

It started in 1891 when Dr. James Naismith used a peach basket and a soccer ball to invent a new game for athletes to play during the period between football and baseball seasons.

He suspended the peach basket above the gymnasium floor and made a game of trying to throw the ball into the basket. So sound was his idea that, from this simple beginning . . .

. . . there developed the modern game of basketball . . . easy to understand, easy to play . . . yet so healthful and stimulating that it has more participants than any other team sport . . . and so thrilling to watch that it can boast greater total attendance than any other sport in the country.

The Y.M.C.A. carried the game around the world. In every civilized country its popularity grew until now it is played in every corner of the globe and its rules have been translated into more than thirty different languages.

Modern basketball is fast, requiring sudden bursts of speed and instant stops that frequently have its players traveling as fast as the fastest sprinters.

o fast that in some situations the ball
s passed at speeds up to 41 miles an
our.

And yet, even at such great speeds, the
game of basketball demands the finest
of control and coordination.

It demands stamina. In a hard game,
and at such speeds, players will often
run as much as 4 or 5 miles during the
course of the game.

And above all, it demands the calm precision and accurate control that enables
a player to find his target quickly in the
rush and pressure of the game and to
shoot accurately over long distances.

A further requirement, and a most essential one is what basketball players call wide angle vision . . . the ability to look straight ahead . . .

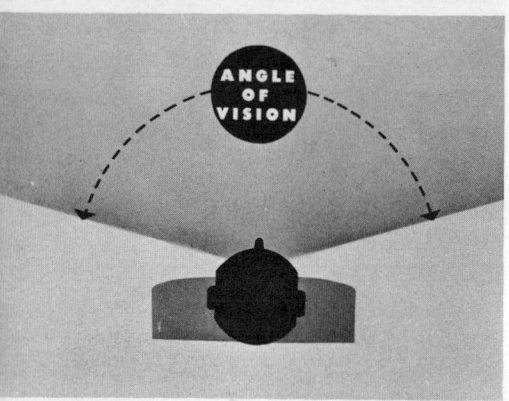

. . . and still see and recognize players on both sides. You must be able to see action on either side without looking at it if you expect to play successful basketball.

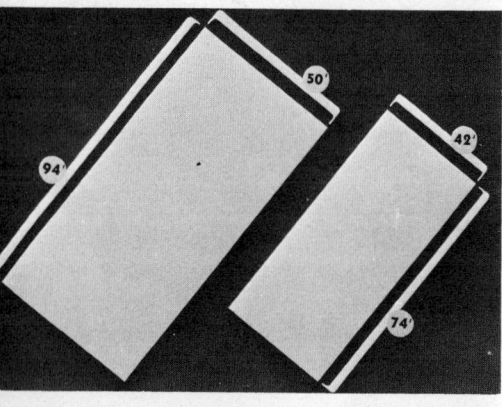

The regulation basketball court is a rectangle with certain maximum and minimum dimensions. The largest a court may be is 94 feet long by 50 feet wide and the smallest, 74 feet long by 42 feet wide. The smaller court is permissible for players of early high school age or younger.

In the middle of each end of the playing area are the basket and backboards. The backboards are inside the court, four feet from the back boundary line.

8

Under each basket is a free throw lane stretching out toward the center of the court and ending in a free throw circle. The lane is twelve feet wide. The center of the circle is fifteen feet from the backboard and the outer edge of the circle is twenty-five feet from the boundary line.

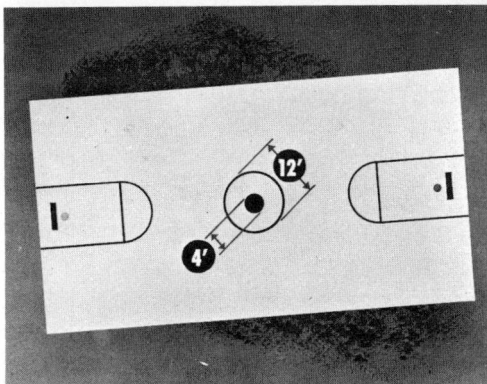

In the exact middle of the court is a circle four feet in diameter, called the center circle. Outside the center circle is another circle twelve feet in diameter called the restraining circle. This is the same size as the free throw circles and all three circles serve the same purpose to keep players back the correct distance on jump balls inside the circles.

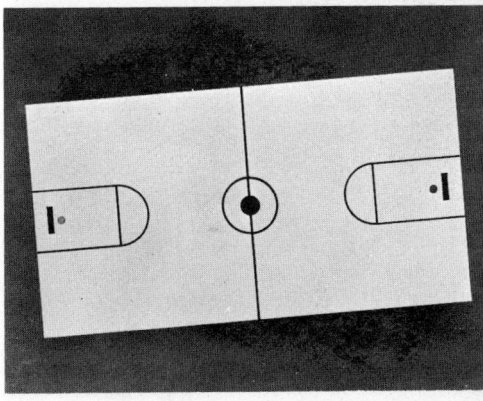

A line across the middle divides the court into two equal parts, called the back court and the front court.

The board behind the basket is made of wood, glass, or metal, and is called the backboard. There are two basic types . . . this square type, six feet wide and four feet high . . .

. . . and this fan shaped backboard. The fan-shaped board is regulation for high school basketball, although the square board is permissible where the gym is already equipped with that type. Transparent backboards are also official for collegiate basketball.

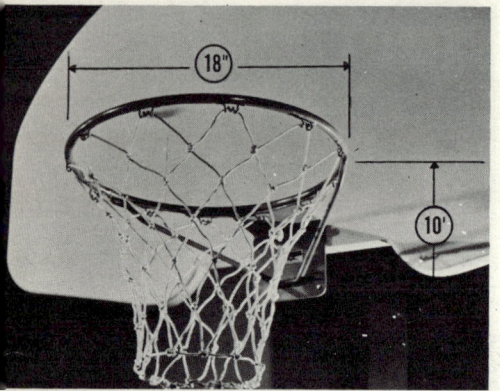

The baskets are white cord nets, open at both ends, suspended from a metal ring eighteen inches in diameter and hung on the backboard ten feet from the floor.

The ball weighs between twenty and twenty-two ounces and holds from seven to nine pounds of air. It may be not less than twenty-nine inches in circumference and not more than thirty.

Personal equipment for basketball is simply shirt, trunks, and sturdy, rubber-soled shoes. Opposing teams usually wear contrasting colors for quick and easy identification during play.

Five men make a basketball team—a center, two forwards and two guards.

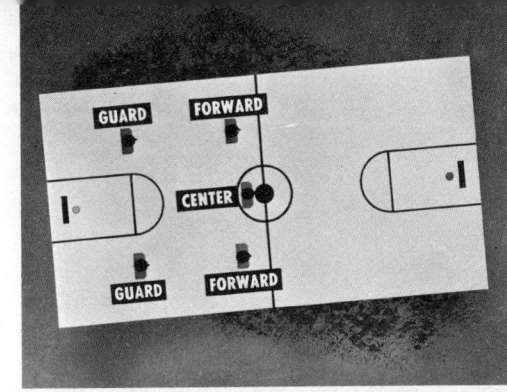

When a game starts each team tries to score in its own basket which is at the opposite end of the floor and the opposing team tries to prevent them from reaching their basket.

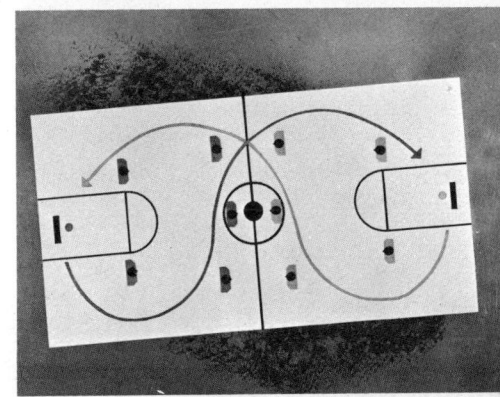

The game is divided into certain time periods. The high school game is made up of four eight minute periods with a two minute intermission between quarters and a ten minute intermission between halves. The college game consists of two twenty-minute periods with a fifteen minute intermission between halves.

The referee puts the ball in play by what is called a center jump. The referee tosses the ball between the two opposing centers and they try to tap the ball toward a team-mate by jumping for it.

When a player gets the ball he must advance it toward his own basket—the one the opposing team is guarding. He must not run with the ball. It's a violation of the rules to take more than one step while either hand is touching the ball.

He can advance the ball by dribbling—that is by running and bouncing the ball as he goes. In this way his hand is not in contact with the ball for more than a single step at a time.

However, if he stops his dribble and touches the ball with both hands, he cannot dribble again. He must get rid of the ball either by passing the ball to a teammate or shooting at the basket.

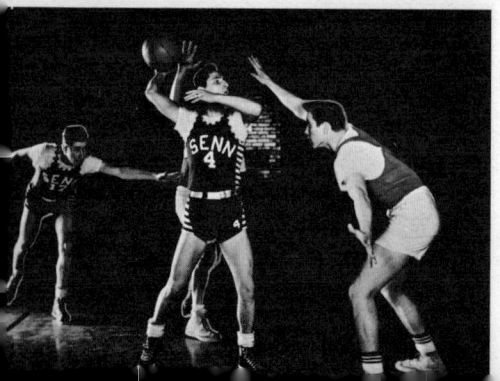

There are no restrictions on how he may pass. He can pass overhand or underhand, with one hand or two hands. He can throw it through the air, bounce it or roll it across the floor, or, he can hand it to a teammate.

And there are no restrictions on shooting. Here, too, he may shoot overhand, underhand, with one hand or two.

A team scores by throwing the ball through its own basket from the top downward. The ball must enter from the top and come out through the bottom. After a score . . .

. . . the ball becomes dead. To put it back in play, the other team takes it out of bounds under the basket and throws or bounces it into the playing area. Then play resumes just as before.

For certain infractions of the rules, the penalty is one or two free throws awarded to the team which was fouled. One player stands behind the line in the free throw circle and tries to throw the ball through his basket.

If he succeeds in getting the ball through the basket on a tree throw, his team scores one point for each successful throw.

1 POINT

On every basket made during play, the team making the basket receives two points. This is known as a Field Goal. The team that scores the most points during the game wins.

2 POINTS

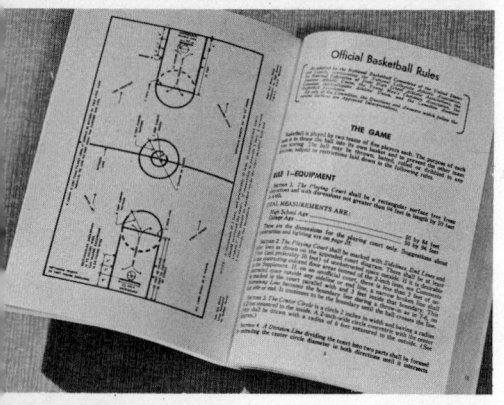

There are many other rules in basketball. They are all explained in the official rule books. Every beginning basketball player should study the rule books until he knows all the rules thoroughly.

Basketball can be one of the fastest, most dazzling of all team sports. It requires excellent team work with perfect coordination between players. But, most important, before that perfect cooperation is possible, every player must be competent in all phases of the game . . . in ball handling, dribbling, passing, shooting, guarding and maneuvering.

14

And he must learn to do all this with a minimum of bodily contact with his opponent. Not roughness, but skill, not brute strength but endurance and stamina are the keys to success in basketball.

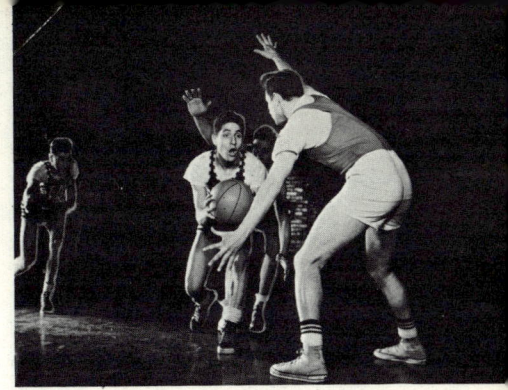

UNIT TWO

IMPROVE YOUR

BALL HANDLING

There are few sports in which there is such unrelenting competition as in basketball. There are no let-downs . . . no coasting periods. During every minute of the game every player's attention is concentrated on gaining possession of the ball.

Since all activity in every game is centered around the ball itself, the first fundamental of winning basketball is skill in ball handling.

By ball handling we mean the position of your hands on the ball and the action of your hands when holding the ball, whether you are preparing to dribble, pass or shoot. It starts, of course, with receiving.

In a game you will have to receive the ball in any number of strained and difficult positions. You have to take it wherever it comes to you. In these cases . . .

. . . no matter what your position of hands and body, your first move, on gaining possession of the ball, should be to get your body under control and the ball properly positioned for play.

Let's begin ball handling with the correct position of hands on the ball. Here is the most effective position—the fingers and thumbs spread evenly around the sides of the ball, the heels of the hands to the rear and both hands a little behind the center of the ball.

And here is one of the most important rules of ball handling—NEVER HOLD THE BALL IN THE PALMS OF YOUR HANDS. Notice how the ball rests on the cushiony part of the fingers and thumbs. Not on the palms. The palms of the hands never touch the ball except for a very brief moment when you receive it.

Now, if you take the ball out of those hands and leave them in exactly the same position, you'll notice . . .

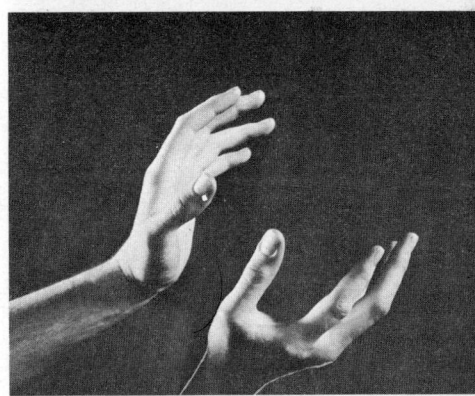

. . . they are positioned like the sides of a funnel. The purpose of this position is to form a backstop for the ball when it comes to you so that hard throws won't go through. The fingers act as a cushion and brake on the ball and serve to trap it when it reaches you.

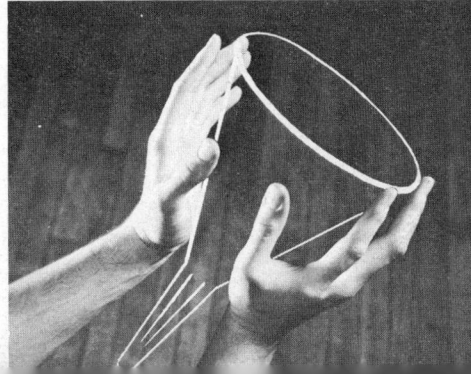

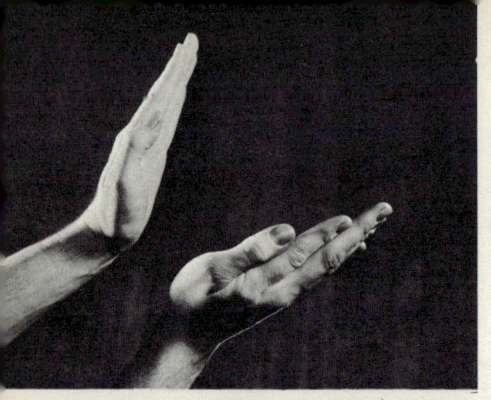

To assume that position, first place your hands in the funnel shape, the heels of your wrists forming the neck of the funnel.

Then relax your hands like this with your fingers and thumbs spread wide apart and your finger tips flexed inward so they will contact the ball first when it is passed to you. With your hands in that position . . .

. . . pick up a ball. It should rest easily on the cushions of your fingers and thumbs . . . not on the palm, at all. And you should have a feeling of firm control. Practice holding the ball this way, moving it around in front of you, until you can feel that control without using the palms of your hands.

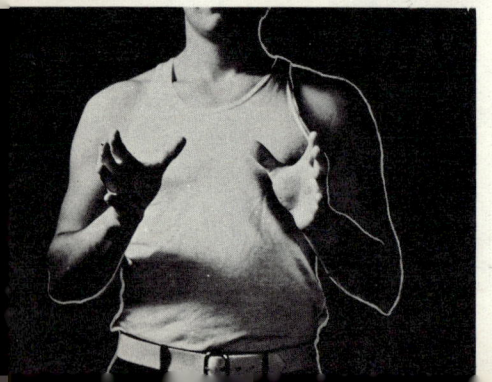

Now let's see the proper action for receiving. There's your hand position from in front. Now imagine a ball is being passed to you from directly in front. That is the most basic pass in the game. By learning it, we can learn all the fundamentals of receiving. To receive it you should move your body toward it.

And there's the complete movement . . . it's a swooping movement forward to meet the ball and then back with the ball as it reaches your hands. Let's try the forward swoop first.

First, bend forward slightly at the waist to get set . . . your hands about waist high in front of you.

Then stride toward the ball, bending your knees and waist in the swooping movement, reaching forward for the ball. Keep your hips low.

Now without stopping, begin the recoil movement after the ball reaches your hands . . . push back with your forward foot and bring your hands back toward your body.

That's all there is to the fundamental movement of receiving. Swoop forward to meet the ball and recoil back with it. Practice this complete movement until it flows easily without any jerking or stabbing. Don't grab at the ball . . . just move forward to meet it and come back with it.

Now let's try it with the ball. As the ball comes toward you, you'll sense the moment to start the forward swooping movement.

Continue in stride and time your movement so that the ball is just out of reach when your arms are fully extended forward.

And that's the moment, just before the ball reaches your hand, that you start your recoil movement. You start back before the ball reaches you and let it catch up with you. Now all your movement is backward, with the ball.

And you cushion the ball in your fingers during that backward movement.

There's the complete movement. Stride forward and reach toward the ball. Start back just before it reaches your hands. And catch it on the way back. Don't stab or grab. It's an easy flowing movement that will become natural to you with practice. But remember this is the fundamental movement of receiving a pass from straight in front.

In actual play, passes won't always come to you from a direct front position. However, no matter what direction they come from and no matter what position you have to get into to receive them . . .

. . . the same fundamentals apply. Reach toward the ball as it comes to you . . . start back before it reaches you and continue back in a recoil movement after it comes into your hands.

And always, as quickly as possible, get back to this correct ball handling position. Here you're ready to pass, dribble or shoot and, if you always start from this position you won't signal your play to your opponents.

Since basketball is a game of continuous action, most of your catches will be made while you are in motion. Here is where you have to consider the direction of your movement. When you receive a ball on the run . . .

. . . you should try to be facing it and moving toward it whenever possible. But it isn't always possible.

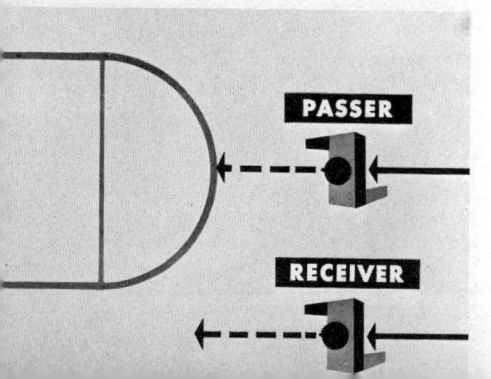

For instance, when you're running parallel with the passer. Here the receiver can't move directly toward the ball.

He should change his direction slightly . . . swing inward toward the ball — to shorten the distance the ball has to travel and thus lessen the chance that a nimble-footed opponent might steal it.

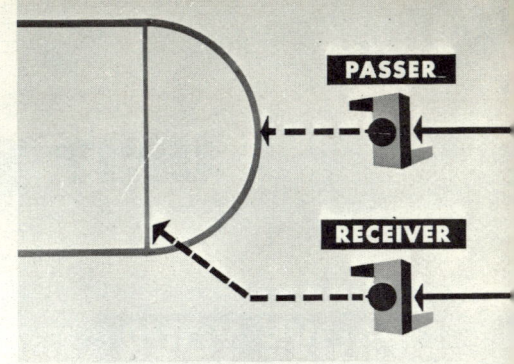

And, on receiving, his shoulders should be turned toward the ball as much as possible.

Ball handling is fundamental in basketball. Without this skill, basketball will be a difficult game for you.

So study these basic movements and practice them until they are instinctive. When you have mastered them, you will be well on your way to winning basketball.

UNIT THREE

IMPROVE YOUR

PASSING

In Basketball no one player can expect . . . nor should he try . . . to score by his own efforts alone. Most of the play consists of passing the ball between players and gradually working it down the floor and into scoring position.

When a player with the ball finds his progress obstructed by an opposing player, he passes to a team-mate in the clear who, in turn passes when his progress is stopped.

It's this constant exchanging of the ball that makes basketball the fast game it is. Thus skill at passing is important to every player. There are many types of passes. Let's study the fundamentals of some of the passes most used.

This is the chest, or push, pass . . . probably used more than any other type of pass in the game. In the chest pass you simply push the ball forward from your chest with a forward thrusting movement of your arms and body. Let's analyze the arm movement first.

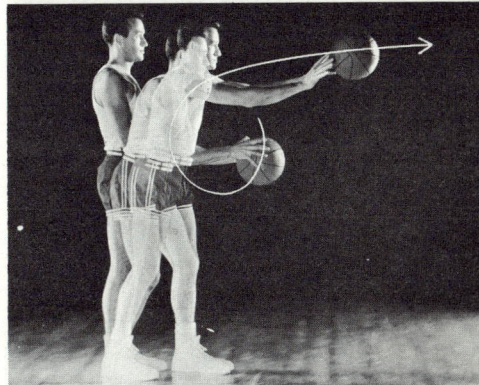

There's the starting position. Ball about chest high, hands a little behind the center of the ball and your fingers spread around the ball's surface. The first movement is downward.

To start the pass smoothly, drop your hands in a small circle, away from you and back up toward the original position.

On the way back, in this preliminary swing, you pass through your original starting position. But don't stop here. Keep the movement flowing smoothly and change direction. From here . . .

. . . just push the ball forward, straight toward the receiver. Don't snap it or throw it. Just push. And try to prevent the ball from spinning as it leaves your hands.

CHEST OR PUSH PASS

There is the complete arm movement. Practice it until it feels smooth and you have control. Then try it coordinated with the proper foot movement.

In the starting position, your feet are parallel.

As you start your preliminary downward swing, step forward with whichever foot is more natural. Now your weight should be evenly distributed on both feet.

As the preliminary swing continues, bend your knees slightly into a slight crouch, ready to put the strength of your legs into the pass too.

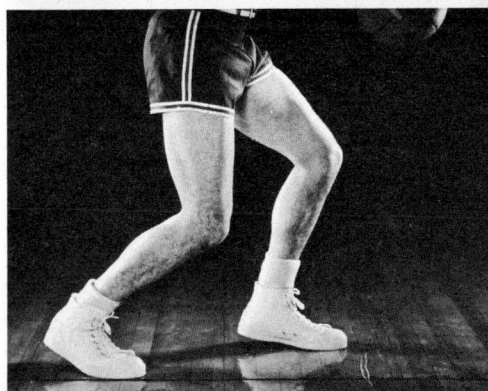

And as you pass, straighten your knees, bringing your weight onto your forward foot as your body comes forward with the pass. As you complete the pass your weight is well forward and your arms are straight out in front of you in the direction of the pass.

This over-the-shoulder pass is most effective for long passes or for fast, hard passes. Essentially, it consists of two basic movements — somewhat like a catcher's snap throw in baseball. First, you bring the ball back over your shoulder to a position behind your right ear; then you throw it forward with a pushing movement, keeping the right hand behind the ball throughout the entire movement.

OVER-THE SHOULDER PASS

Let's try the arm movement first. Here's your starting position . . . the fundamental ball handling position. From here you start by bringing the ball back into a cocked position behind your ear.

There's the movement. Bring the ball back the shortest and fastest way — straight back. And at the cocked position, just before your arm starts forward, your right forearm should be approximately perpendicular. During this movement . . .

. . . the left hand stays against the ball, balancing it against the right until about this position. Sometimes you may hold this position for an instant until your receiver is in the clear. Then back to the cocked position and start the ball forward.

It's a full body movement, from the feet up as your body pivots into the pass and your arm straightens forward. In the final push, just let the ball leave your hand with a full hand extension and follow through with your arm outstretched after the ball. Now, let's see how this arm movement is coordinated with the movement of feet and body.

28

There's your starting position, just as you receive the ball and bring it under control. Your weight is fairly evenly balanced on both feet. Now, as you bring the ball back to the cocked position . . .

. . . your left shoulder turns toward the receiver. Step back with your right foot—quarter turn back to the right—and carry your weight back onto the right foot. Now, your weight is well back, ready to move forward with the pass.

As you start the ball forward, your weight goes forward too, adding the power of your legs and body to the pass. At about this point in your pass your weight has shifted completely to your left foot and as you continue forward . . .

You step forward with your right foot. Now you pivot slightly on your left foot; your shoulders come 'round with the pass.

There's the complete forward movement of feet and body for the over-the-shoulder pass with one hand. Notice how the shoulders pivot behind the pass as your forward stride and body movement adds power to your pass.

Study this pass and practice it from both the right and left side . . . a good passer must be able to pass from either side. It's a two-count rhythm . . . the first count quick as the ball comes back . . . then a quick reversal and the throw with feet, body, shoulders and arms.

This is the two hand underhand pass, used mostly after a stop or a pivot but often useful for any short or medium length pass. It can be made either from the right or left side of the body depending on the position of the receiver and your opponent.

2 HAND UNDERHAND PASS

There are the basic movements — first the ball drawn back to a position close to your hip — then passed — not thrown — forward with both hands. Both hands have an equal part in the pass and both hands leave the ball together.

As you start the pass, ball and feet move simultaneously. Bring the ball back beside your hip and step forward with the opposite foot, bending your knees into a semi-crouch position. If you're passing the ball from your right hip step forward with your left foot and vice versa.

At the end of this backswing your right hand is slightly behind your left and your right elbow is cocked back behind you. From here both hands bring the ball forward . . .

. . . rotating the ball slightly until, when the ball is just in front of you, your hands are even — neither is very much ahead of the other. As you swing the ball forward, your weight starts forward too.

Both hands follow the ball all the way out and the ball leaves both hands simultaneously.

And you follow through with both hands extended and your weight fully forward, leaning into the pass. Let the ball slide off the ends of your fingers naturally.

The two handed underhand pass is a simple movement, useful as a hand-off or for short, quick passes. And you should be able to perform it well either from the right hip like this . . .

. . . or from the left hip, like this. You'll need skill in passing from both sides to elude guards working close to you.

1 HAND UNDERHAND PASS

This one hand underhand pass is exactly the same as the two hand underhand pass except that during the forward swing the right hand stays behind the ball; the left comes away and the right hand only follows through.

Up to this point — the end of the backswing — it is exactly the same as the two hand underhand pass. Now, as the forward swing starts, the left hand stays in front, leading the swing until the ball is just in front of the body.

At this point, the left hand leaves the ball entirely and swings off to the left while the right hand stays behind the ball, pushing it forward toward the receiver.

And the follow-through is with the right hand only — the arm fully extended and the weight well forward on the left foot.

BOUNCE PASS

The bounce pass is a method of getting the ball past guards where other passes would be blocked. You simply bounce the ball to the receiver instead of throwing it. This pass should start from an underhand or low chest position because a higher starting position would increase the distance the ball has to travel, thus giving your opposition more time to block it.

Here is a bounce pass developing out of what started as a two hand underhand pass. All the fundamentals are the same until the ball is just in front of you on the forward swing. But now, instead of passing straight out in front of you . . .

You change direction slightly and bounce the ball to the receiver. This type of pass requires more finger control than ordinary push passes.

There are many other types of passes in basketball, for instance, this hook pass, but those we have discussed are the basic passes. Learn and practice those well, and the others will come to you easily and naturally when you are ready for them.

UNIT FOUR

IMPROVE YOUR

DRIBBLING

So far we have emphasized the basic techniques of good control of the ball . . . so essential to playing winning basketball.

Now, in dribbilng, it's time to learn the second fundamental basketball skill — control of the body in possession of the ball.

For only with perfect poise and constant body balance is the dribbler able to maintain posession of the ball against alert opposition.

Dribbling is basically an arm-wrist-finger action — and there is the starting position — your body slightly bent forward, knees relaxed and your forearm parallel with the floor . . . your arm as relaxed as possible. From this position . . .

. . . move your forearm upward about five inches with your wrist and fingers well relaxed . . .

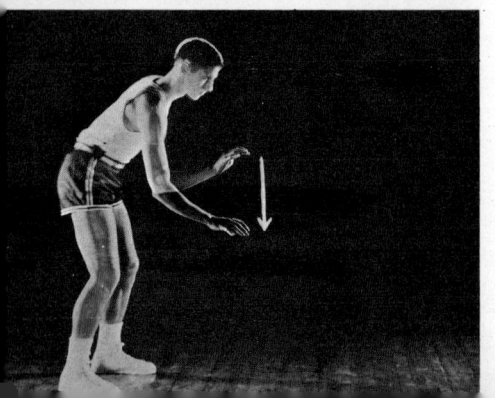

. . . then back down about a foot. Keep your upper arm steady, moving your forearm on the elbow joint with your fingers and wrist relaxed.

And that's the dribble movement — easy, relaxed, up and down, with a relaxed but controlled wrist. It isn't a slapping movement . . . more of a pushing down with the spread fingers and drawing back up again. Practice this movement until it feels smooth and rhythmic with each hand. Then . . .

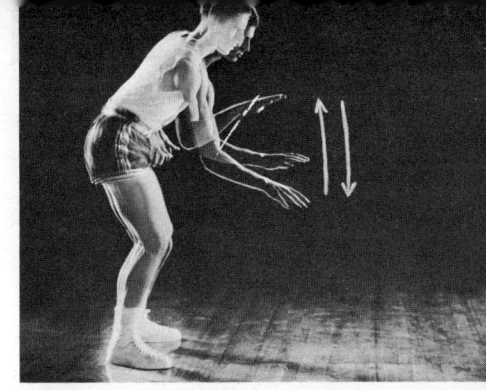

. . . using the same relaxed motion, start bouncing the ball on the floor. Don't slap the ball down . . . just push it down . . .

. . . and let your hand ride back up with it. After the downward push hold your hand down and wait for the ball. Then let your fingers and hand ride back up with it.

Then simply push it back down again. Your fingers should be in contact with the ball for as long as possible during the upward and downward movements. That way you keep better control.

Now try the same thing with the other hand and practice the dribble until you have perfect control with both hands and without looking at the ball. Focus your eyes on the floor a few feet in front of you and when you've mastered the dribble standing still . . .

. . . start moving forward, dribbling as you go. Try to keep your eyes off the ball. If you look at the ball, you cannot see what the other players are doing. Move slowly at first.

Notice that now, instead of pressing the ball straight down, you have to push it slightly forward to keep it ahead of your moving body. When you can walk slowly forward and dribble without looking at the ball . . .

. . . change hands and master the dribble with the other hand. Don't try to travel fast until the coordination of legs and arm is completely natural.

It should be apparent, however, that while you are in this upright position, the ball is relatively unprotected. It would be easy for an opposing guard to snatch it away from you as it makes that long trip from your hand to the floor.

To protect the ball better, keep low — shorten the distance between your hand and the floor. Without the ball, crouch low like a sprinter at the start of a race . . .

. . . and practice moving around with your body close to the floor.

Then, keeping your body low, try dribbling. In this position, with your hand working so close to your knees, you'll have to be particularly careful about the distance you keep the ball ahead of you.

If you dribble too close, the ball will hit your knees, bounce away, and you'll lose it.

If you dribble too far ahead of you it will be difficult to control. Through practice you'll find the best distance between you and the ball at all speeds and in all body positions.

As you gain skill and start to pick up speed, you will raise your body higher from the crouched position, providing you're in the clear. But when you're threatened . . .

. . . you'll drop back to the crouch position because that way you have best protection.

Notice how your hunched-over body protects that ball. And the shorter the distance the ball has to travel from your hand to the floor, the less the danger of losing it to an opponent.

Keep both arms well in front of you. You'll find a tendency to let the arm not being used for dribbling drop down to the side. But keep it up and ahead of you.

You'll need it to ward off opponents and to recover the ball if it should be knocked out of your control.

In dribbling, as in passing, wide angle vision will be one of your most valuable assets. With good wide-angle vision, you should be able to identify players at almost ninety degrees from your forward direction.

If you look in the direction you're going to move, you signal your intention and you'll probably be blocked.

But if you keep your eyes on the floor in front of you, just over the top of your working hand, you'll be able to see openings and teammates without looking at them and your opponents will never know your next move.

Dribbling is one of basketball's essential skills. All it takes is a knowledge of the fundamentals and plenty of practice.

UNIT FIVE

IMPROVE YOUR

PIVOTING

One of the important maneuvers that helps make basketball such a highly competitive sport is the pivot, which gives the offensive player a means of meeting and avoiding the defensive tactics of an energetic guard.

When you pivot, you come to a stop and swing around on one foot; then either shoot for the basket, dribble, or pass to a teammate to get the ball out of danger. The main thing is to protect the ball by placing your body between the ball and opposing guard.

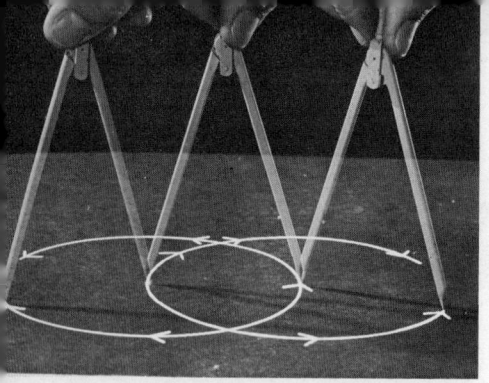

And a pivoting player is much like a pair of dividers. Just as dividers pivot on one of their two points and swing through complete circles . . .

. . . So a basketball player pivots on one or the other foot, through a complete circle or as much of the circle as he wants, without lifting that pivot foot off the floor. The rules define legal and illegal pivots so let's examine them first.

The simplest pivot rule applies to a player who receives the ball while standing still with both feet on the floor.

That man may pivot in either direction on his left foot . . .

. . . or he may pivot in either direction on his right foot. He has his choice.

But supposing that player caught the ball while moving with one foot in the air and decided to pivot and either pass or shoot. He would have to stop when that foot in the air came to the ground.

That's called a two-count stop . . . when you receive the ball with one foot in the air and one on the floor. Count one as you catch the ball . . . count two as your other foot comes to the ground.

2 COUNT STOP

In this case your rear foot is your pivot foot. On a two-count stop your rear foot must be your pivot foot.

2 COUNT STOP

PIVOT FOOT

And you can pivot around on that foot as long as you want to as long as you don't lift that pivot foot off the floor.

Now here's an exception to that two-count stop rule. This is a two count stop, but the other foot came down exactly parallel with the first one. In this case . . .

. . . you could pivot on either foot, just as if you had caught the ball standing still with both feet on the ground.

This is another type of stop — called a one-count stop. The player caught the ball while he was in the air, with both feet off the ground. Both feet come down together in a single count after he has caught the ball.

46

In this case he can pivot on either foot just as though he had been standing still. Those are the basic rules of pivoting. Let's review them.

On a one count stop, either foot may be the pivot foot.

On a two-count stop, the rear foot is always the pivot foot . . . unless . . .

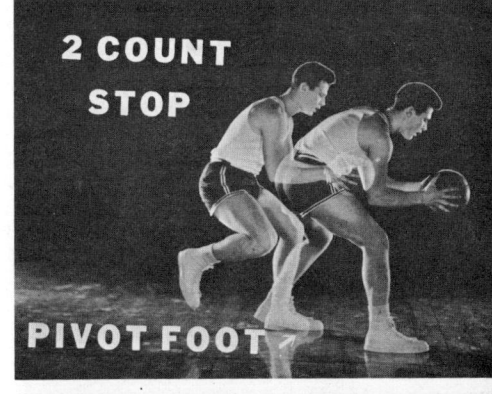

. . . the second foot comes down exactly parallel with the first. Then either foot is the pivot foot.

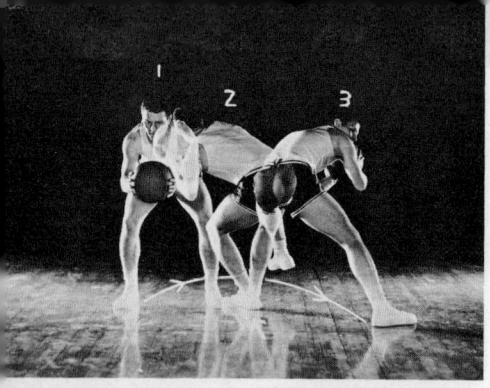

Now let's see how to use these pivots and turns in play. This is a reverse pivot, where you pivot back away from your opponent.

As you meet your opponent in this situation, the ball is exposed. If you pass to the right or left, the chances are he'll be able to reach the ball. So you decide to pivot and pass to the right.

Your right foot is your pivot foot and you swing your body back around to the left. Now your shoulder is coming between the ball and your opponent. Keep swinging around to the left . . .

. . . until your back is to your opponent, your whole body between him and the ball.

And pass, using your body for protection.

In the same situation you can protect the ball with your shoulder by using a forward cross or turn. Here you receive the ball with your feet parallel, so you can pivot on either foot.

You can swing your left foot forward and across in front of you, bringing your shoulder between your opponent and the ball. Then pass to the right.

Or you can swing your right foot across in front of you . . .

. . . and pass off to the left. Pivots, crosses and turns like this can get you out of trouble quickly and they can often open the way for an offensive play.

A pivot is most useful when it is done with speed and deception. So learn the fundamentals and then practice them thoroughly so that they become an instinctive part of your body control and ball handling during a game.

UNIT SIX

IMPROVE YOUR

SHOOTING

All fundamental skills in basketball are important to the game. But if any one were to be singled out for extra practice, it would be the fundamentals of shooting.

It's the ability to shoot . . . to see the ball sink through the basket on a good percentage of shots . . . that wins games. It makes little difference how well a team dribbles and passes to work the ball into scoring position, unless . . .

. . . every member of the team can coordinate body control and ball control to become good shooters. Let's analyze the fundamentals of some of the most common shots.

CHEST OR PUSH SHOT

One of the most common shots is the chest, or push shot, used mostly for long range shooting. Essentially, the shot uses the same movements as the chest or push pass . . . a short downward and backward swing to get the movement flowing smoothly, then an upward push toward the basket as the knees straighten and push upward simultaneously. Then a forward step for the follow-through.

Here's your starting position . . . ball about chest high, lightly but firmly cushioned in the fingers and thumbs . . . not against the palms. Eyes should be on the target and they must stay there until the ball reaches its destination. Now, start the shot with a downward movement.

Swing the ball down and back in a small smooth loop. The purpose of this preliminary swing is to get the ball in motion smoothly and avoid a sudden push which makes control more difficult. Simultaneously, bend your knees.

Don't move your feet. Just sink your hips slightly to get your body down behind the upward swing.

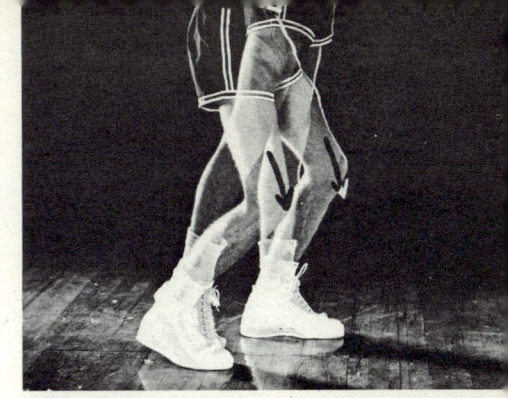

Now, continue the preliminary swing by pushing the ball upward toward the basket in a high looping arc. Push with your arms and . . .

. . . push with your knees and get the power of your legs into the shot. Your rear foot will come completely off the floor during the shot.

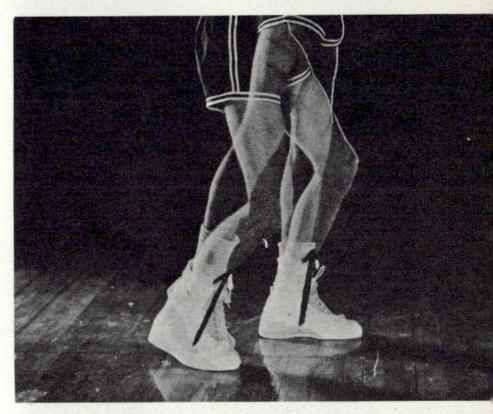

Continue the arm movement, pushing, not throwing, the ball on its way. Follow through with your arms outstretched and your palms toward the basket.

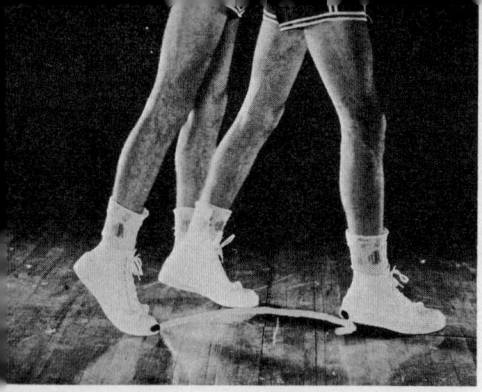

Now, as your weight comes forward with the shot, bring your rear foot forward in a short step to keep your balance and . . .

. . . end in an alert position ready to go in after the rebound if necessary.

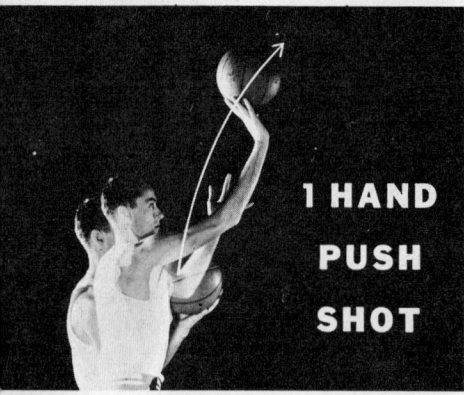

1 HAND PUSH SHOT

The one hand chest, or push, shot is a variation of the two hand shot. Footwork is exactly the same. The difference comes as the ball is carried up from the catching position when one hand drops away from the ball and the other pushes it on toward the basket and follows through.

From the catching position, the movement starts with the same short preliminary swing, down and back to get the action flowing smoothly.

But as the ball comes back up, rotate the ball between your hands to get one hand under the ball and the other behind it— the pushing hand behind and the other underneath. Here the shot will be a right hand shot so the right hand is behind the ball and the left simply holds it in position. From here . . .

. . . simply push with the right hand. As the right hand gets control of the ball let your left hand swing out to the side for balance and . . .

. . . follow through after the ball just as in the two hand push shot, except that here only the pushing hand follows through. Then prepare to go after any rebound.

Another valuable shot is the lay-up shot, or under-the-basket shot, made while you are charging in to score. You simply move toward the basket, leap into the air at a point where your forward momentum will carry you almost under it — but to one side — lay the ball up against the backboard about 18 inches above the rim, from which spot it should carrom into the basket.

Since footwork is the important factor here, let's practice it first. If you are approaching the basket from the right side, you should run in and take off from your left foot.

This puts the body in a natural throwing position for shooting with the right hand, which is the hand to use on the right side of the basket. By using the hand closest to the backboard, you protect the ball.

Now practice coming in to the left side of the basket and leaping with the right foot.

Now the left hand is in a free position to swing the ball upward. The rule to remember is "Opposite foot, opposite hand."

Now practice dribbling with the ball toward the right side of the basket, or practice catching a pass near the basket, and with the ball held in both hands, about waist high, start your jump, bringing the ball upward as you do so.

Both hands push the ball upward as far as possible. Then . . .

. . . at the full extent of both arms let the left hand drop away. Push the ball upward with the right, laying it against the board about 18 inches above the rim. The ball should then carrom back through the basket.

Now practice the same basic movements, but approaching the basket from the left side, leaping from the floor with the right foot and shooting with the left hand. In all cases, this should be a graceful, easy-flowing movement.

If you approach the basket directly from the front, don't try to lay it against the board but on an imaginary shelf about 18 inches above the front portion of the rim so that the ball drops through the rim without touching the backboard.

PIVOT OR HOOK SHOT

A basic shot that every player should learn is the pivot or hook shot. As you receive the ball with your back to the basket, you turn to your left, spot the basket quickly, and lay the ball up against the backboard with your right hand.

Start the motion with the ball held in approximate receiving position. Your feet will usually be parallel to each other. In play you may want to draw your guard off balance with a feint to the right but . . .

. . . your first shooting movement is to your left with your left foot . . . a step around toward the basket as your body starts to pivot.

Next, shift your weight to your left foot, as you swing your body around to the left.

At almost the same moment, spot the basket, and bring the ball up in a wide, over-the-head sweeping movement and shoot to lay the ball against the backboard.

As your body carries around to face the basket after your shot, your weight comes back into balance on both feet.

Naturally, this shot may be made by turning right instead of left, and using the left hand, after shifting the weight to the right foot.

Many basketball games are won by the free throw, so every player should know its fundamentals and be able to use them well. This shot is usually made with a two-hand underhand, or pull, motion from a position directly behind the foul line.

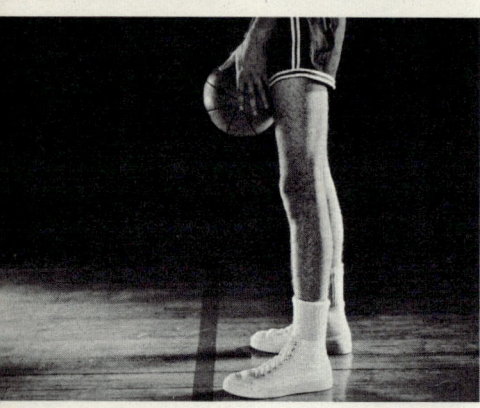

The toe of the forward foot should be placed about an inch back from the foul line, although you may find it more comfortable to stand with feet parallel.

For an accurate free throw, the ball must be centered in the hands. Find the center spot by spinning it between the two index fingers, guiding its motion with the thumbs. When it twirls evenly, without pulling in any direction, you will have found the exact center.

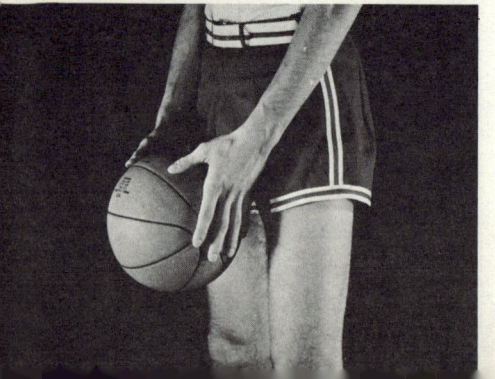

Now spread the fingers, evenly, around the ball, a little to the rear. In this spot, more than in any of the others, the muscles of arms and hands must be thoroughly relaxed, except for what pressure is necessary to hold the ball.

Now you are ready to make the throw. As you get set, you may be conscious of extreme nervous tension. A deep breath, held for a few seconds, will help in slowing down the heart action and calming your nerves.

Begin the throwing motion by bending the knees in a slight crouch. With your arms straight, the ball is dropped to a position between your knees. Your weight should rest on the balls of your feet.

Now bring the ball upward with your arms in a wide, extended arc, and at the same time, rise up from your crouch.

On the follow-through you should look as if you were taking a long upward and slightly forward stretch after the ball. The palms should be facing inward and forward, hands about a foot apart.

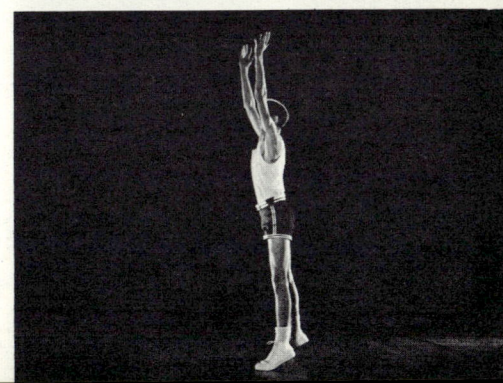

The ball should travel in a medium arc constant arch to the basket and drop through the rim.

There is no easy road to accurate shooting. You may be born a good shooter with natural body control that will go long way toward making you an accurate marksman. But practice alone will give you the confidence without which you will never be able to shoot consistently under game pressure.

UNIT SEVEN

IMPROVE YOUR

DEFENSE

So far in this series we have studied the techniques of advancing the ball and scoring. In other words we have studied offense. But offense is only half of the game.

Of equal importance are the techniques of defense; for, no matter how fast and accurate your team may be, your score won't mean much if you can't keep your opponents from scoring as well or better. There are three strategic types of defense.

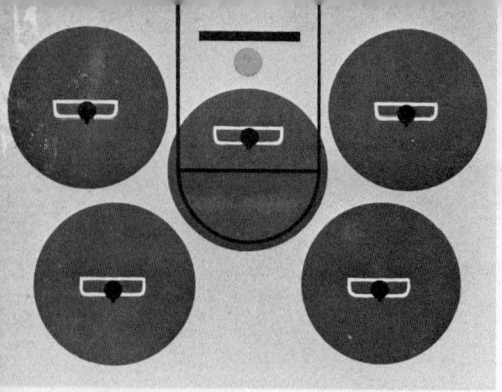

First, zone defense, in which each player is responsible for a certain zone on the floor and each guards any opponent who enters that zone.

Second, man-to-man, or individual, defense. Here each player is assigned a certain opposing player and he guards that player no matter where he goes on the floor. There are many combinations of these two systems but they are all just variations of these two basic plans.

No matter what types of defense your team uses, success depends on how well every player does his individual job. Defense of any kind is based on fundamentals that concern the individual alone, so we can learn best by studying man-to-man defense.

The best stance for defense is the one that gives you the greatest mobility. You should be ready to move in any direction instantly. And you should try to make your arms and body cover as great an area as possible.

Start your practice of the stance by placing your feet like a boxer's . . . one foot slightly ahead of the other, feet well spread and your weight well up on the balls of your feet.

Then bend your knees and let your hips sink and spread your arms wide. You can keep your arms extended sideways like this if you wish.

This sideways spread gives your opponent an impression of a very wide obstacle to go around and from here you can raise or lower your arms to offset any tactics he may use.

Or, in some instances, you may want to have one hand up and the other out to the side.

The advantage of this position is that your upraised hand is ready to block overhead shots or passes while the other is in position to thrust at the ball or block low passes. If you use this stance you should practice alternating hands so that you can guard just as effectively with either hand held up.

The third effective arm position is with both hands out in front below shoulder height. This is probably the most natural of the three.

In this position you can make cat-like thrusts at the ball and raise or lower your hands quickly if your opponent passes.

You'll probably use all three positions at different times so you should be proficient in all of them. But, whatever your position, keep moving. Keep your arms moving and move your body to present as difficult an obstacle as possible.

A moving guard distracts a player and makes it difficult for him to concentrate on his passing or shooting. So keep moving.

A guard's footwork is like the footwork of a boxer. Always keep your feet apart and don't walk or run when you're guarding close — shuffle with short quick steps.

There's the forward footwork in diagram form. The forward foot moves forward first. Then the rear foot comes up behind. Then the front foot forward again. And the rear foot up behind. You never cross your legs and your forward foot stays forward.

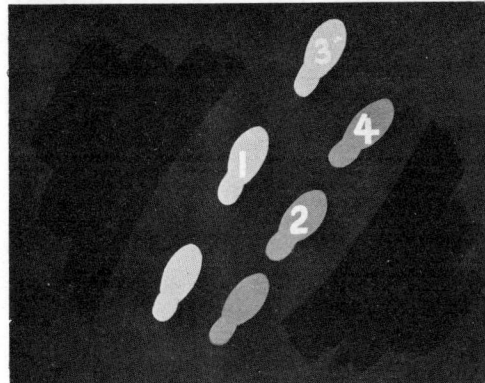

To move backward, you simply reverse the process. First your rear foot slides back; then your front foot comes back after it. Then the rear foot again and then the front foot.

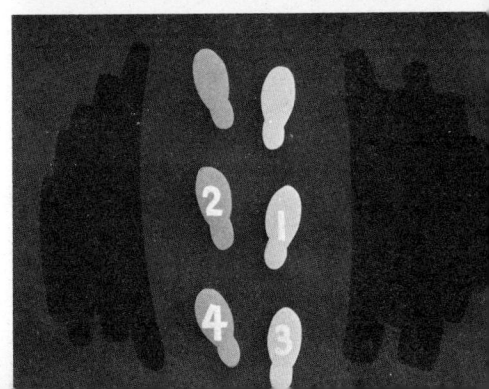

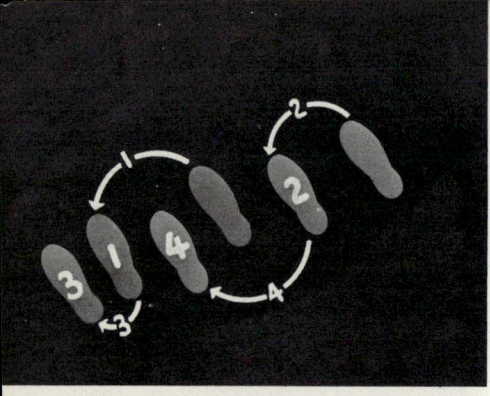

To move sideways, it's the same shuffle. If you want to move to the left, your left foot moves first; then the right foot follows. In defensive basketball, never cross your legs.

You may be tempted to take a running step to catch up with a fast player, but if you do, here's what happens. If your opponent suddenly changes direction, you're off balance and you'll probably be left two or three steps behind.

And don't lunge or take long steps toward your opponent like this. A smart offensive player will make his break or cut around you while you are in the middle of the lunge. Before you can recover you've lost him.

Ideally, your job on defense is to prevent your opponent from getting any closer to the basket than when he receives the ball. The only way you can do this is to confront him with an obstacle to his forward progress so your best position on defense is between your opponent and his basket.

When he comes toward you with the ball you must decide whether to rush in and meet him or wait for him to come to you.

If he's coming in at full speed, drop back toward the basket and get started in the same direction he's coming. At the same time try to crowd him toward the sideline and, if possible, force him out of bounds.

But if he's approaching slowly, go out and meet him, arms outstretched, and block his progress.

He'll very likely try to go around you, first feinting one way to throw you off balance and then cutting around you in the opposite direction.

To get around you he'll have to travel in a wide arc. The temptation for you will be to try to follow close beside him in a smaller arc of your own. However, this would be a mistake.

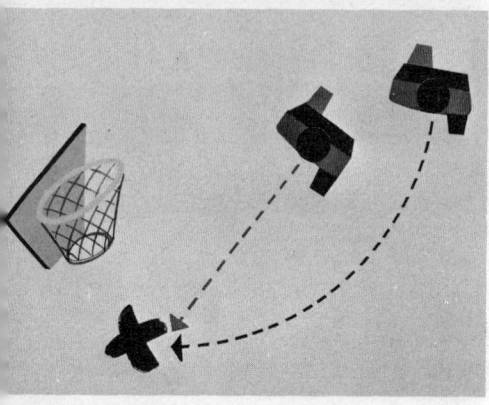

What you should do is break in a straight line for a spot that will put you between the dribbler and the basket. Here the dribbler, represented by the black line cuts in a wide arc. The guard cuts straight toward a point where he can meet the dribbler again and place an obstacle in his path toward the basket.

If you do this, in most cases your opponent will be forced to stop and either pass back or shoot under great difficulty.

Occasionally, you may feel in a position to bat the ball away from the dribbler. But you will find that in most cases the effort will throw you out of balance and out of step so that the dribbler is able to get around you.

You will find that if you simply concentrate on keeping your proper defensive position — that is, between the dribbler and the basket — you will be doing enough. After the dribbler has been stopped, he can only pass or shoot, and you should be in a position to interfere with either movement.

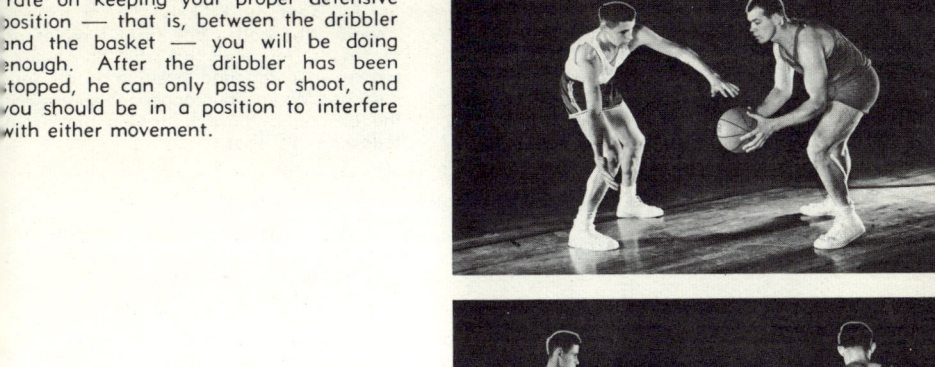

When the player you are guarding does not have the ball, you should still maintain your defensive position between him and the basket although you may play him "loose" — that is you don't have to stay as close to him as you do when he has the ball. This "loose" position gives you a better chance to see both the opponent **and** the ball.

And when the ball comes toward your man, you can move in quickly.

In team play other offensive men may interfere with your defense so you must be aware of actions of other offensive players as well.

You must also be ready to take the offense whenver the opportunity presents itself. Your most likely chance for recovering the ball, aside from fumbles, is in taking rebounds off the backboard. Hence your rebound position is all important. When your opponent shoots for the basket, prepare to screen him from following his shot.

Don't turn to face the basket immediately, but watch him until he shows what direction he will take.

Then turn to block him out, pick up the flight of the ball and go in after it.

As we said before, the key to all success in defensive play is mental alertness. Because the defensive player cannot know what action to expect from his opponent, he must be ready for anything. But after all, that's one of the things that makes basketball one of the world's favorite sports.

HISTORY OF BASKETBALL

Basketball is a comparatively modern game, having been introduced to the world in 1891 by Dr. James A. Naismith, who invented the game while working as physical director of the Y.M.C.A. in Springfield, Mass. The first official game of basketball was played on January 20, 1892. It is strictly an American game, being distinct in most or all respects from any sporting games played before its invention.

Dr. Naismith invented the game in an effort to find some sport which could be played indoors, and which had the team play, the thrills, and the physical benefits of football, without football's rough bodily contact.

The first baskets to be used in basketball were exactly that — two peach baskets hung at opposite ends of the gymnasium. The first games were played with 7 men on a side. This number was changed to 9, then to 8, and finally to the present-day 5. In the game's infancy, field goals were scored as 3 points. Each team had a special "foul shooter" who attempted all free throws for the rest of his team. Games were played in 3 periods of 20 minutes each.

Although the rules of basketball were formulated so that "elderly" people might enjoy some form of team recreation, the game was quickly adopted by young people, despite the fact that many persons regarded the game as sissified and tried to prove their contention by picking fights with basketball players.

But this feeling soon died as the high speed and precision of the game attracted more and more people to it. The game spread quickly throughout the East, and then, as schools realized its potentialities, all throughout the country. Basketball had international appeal, too; before the First World War, the game was being played with fervor in practically every country on earth. It was estimated that before 1941, some 20,000,000 persons were playing the game all over the globe. Today, basketball ranks close to softball as being the nation's No. 1 spectator sport.

Until 1915, basketball was pretty much confined, despite its popularity, to being a gymnasium exercise, for, with the exception of a few professional leagues which sprang up and died, the game had little or no organization. It seemed that everyone played under a different set of rules, and the resulting confusion hampered the real growth of the game. In 1915, however, three amateur organizations, the National Collegiate Athletic Association, the Amateur Athletic Union, and the Y.M.C.A., met to discuss and formulate a common set of rules. This crystalization of rules gave the game the boost needed to bring it to its present heights. Today, basketball is played in practically every town and hamlet in America, by boys and girls alike. Every year, millions of people flock to thrill in the furious action, the precision shooting, the great team play that has made basketball the wonderful sport that it is.

SOME RULES OF BASKETBALL

The Playing Area

Basketball may be played indoors or out of doors, although in America it is generally an indoor game. Basketball is played on a court ranging in size from a maximum of 94 feet long by 50 feet wide to a minimum of 74 feet long by 42 feet wide. Ideal measurements are:

College Age..94 by 50 feet
High School Age...84 by 50 feet
Junior High School Age..74 by 42 feet

The court is to have a hard surface, usually of wood. There should at least be 3 feet (preferably 10) of unobstructed space on all sides of the court.

At either end of the court there are backboards made of wood, glass, steel or other rigid, flat materials. The backboards must be one of two types: a rectangle 6 feet long and 4 feet high, or a fan-shaped board. The front face of the backboard is to be four feet in from the end boundary line, and parallel with it. The basket is attached to the center of the backboard so that the rim of the basket is 10 feet from the floor. From the basket ring is suspended a white cord net.

In the exact center of the court is a circle, 4 feet in diameter, known as the center circle. A "restraining circle," 12 feet in diameter, is concentric with the center circle.

At the center at each end of the court there are free throw lanes, 12 feet wide, ending in circles 12 feet in diameter. The centers of these circles are to be 19 feet from the end boundary lines. A "free throw line" is drawn through the circle, parallel with the end boundary line. The free throw line is 15 feet from the plane of the face of the backboard.

A "division line" divides the court into two equal parts. A team's "front court" is that part of the court containing the team's own basket, that is, the basket through which a team tries to score its points. The other half of the court is known as that team's "back court". For an opposing team, the names are reversed.

The Ball

A basketball is to be round, no larger than 30 inches in circumference and no smaller than 29. Its weight should be no more than 22 ounces nor less than 20 ounces. When inflated, it should bounce to a height (measured to top of ball) of not less than 49 inches nor more than 54 inches after it has been dropped from a height of six feet (measured to bottom of ball). The home team is to provide the basketball for any game.

The Team

A basketball team consists of 5 players, generally known as a center, two forwards and two guards. A team cannot begin a game with less than five players, but if it has no substitutes to replace disqualified players, it must finish the game with less than five players. Under current rules, a player must leave the game after committing five personal fouls, and cannot return during that game. Each player should wear a numbered shirt.

The Officials

The officials should be a Referee and an Umpire, assisted by two Timers and two Scorers. A single Timer and a single Scorer may be used if acceptable to both teams. Officials must conduct the game according to the rules.

Scorers record personal and technical fouls, and notify the Referee when the fifth personal foul is called on a player. They also record time-outs charged against each team. In keeping track of the scoring, most officials use the following symbols:

P1, P2, P3, etc. for personal fouls;

T for technical fouls;

O for free throw attempt, X inside the O if try is good;

2 for field goals.

A field goal counts two points. A successful free throw counts 1 point.

Game Times

Teams of college age play two 20-minute halves, with a 15 minute intermission between the halves.

Teams of high school age play four 8-minute quarters, with two 1-minute intermissions between the quarters and a 10-minute intermission between the halves.

For teams of less than high school age, the quarters are 6 minutes, with 2-minute intermissions between quarters and a 10-minute intermission at half time.

Overtime Periods

If the score is tied at the end of the second half in games of college-age levels, play shall continue for an extra period of 5 minutes, or for as many extra 5-minutes periods as are needed to break the tie. A 2-minute intermission is taken before each extra period. The ball is put in play at the center circle at the start of each extra period.

In games of high school age level or below, games which end in ties at the end of regulation time are played off in extra periods of 3 minutes each, with a 2-minute intermission before each extra period. If a team is ahead by 1 point or more at the end of any extra period, it wins. As soon as a team accumulates 2 points after the first extra period, the game is immediately over, and that team wins.

Time-Outs

Each team is allowed five charged time-outs during regular play. A charged time-out is either a time-out requested by a player when the ball is dead or that player's team has control of the ball; or a time-out for an injury or removal of a disqualified player, except that a time-out is not charged if an injured or disqualified player is replaced within 1½ minutes. If the officials halt a game to permit a player to tie a shoelace, a time-out is not charged.

Some Other Rules

Visiting teams have the choice of baskets for the first half. Teams change baskets for the second half.

The score of a forfeited game is 2 to 0.

When a team gains control of the basketball in its back court, it must move the ball into its front court within 10 seconds, unless the ball is touched by an opponent. When that happens, a new play starts, with a new 10-second period allowed.

SOME COMMON BASKETBALL TERMS

Advancing Figure of Eight: An attempt by ball handlers to move ball toward the basket, following a figure-eight pattern.

Back Court: The half of the court containing basket a team is defending, including the division line itself.

Basket: Metal ring 18" in diameter attached to backboard 10' above and parallel to the floor.

Basket-Hanging: Remaining under opponents' basket while opponents have the ball in the other territory.

Blind Pass: Looking in one direction and passing ball in another, using split vision.

Brush-Off: Getting rid of a defensive player by forcing him to run into one of your teammates.

Cage: To score a basket.

Charging: A violent and unnecessary contact with an opponent. It is a personal foul.

Clean Shot: A shot that goes through the hoop without touching backboard.

Crip Shot: An easy short shot, close to basket, made without interference.

Decoy Cut: A cut calculated to free a teammate from being guarded.

Drag: A dribble in which the ball is dribbled at the side of the body to keep it away from a guarding opponent.

Dribble: To move the ball by throwing, bouncing, batting, or rolling. Dribbling is terminated if player touches ball simultaneously with both hands or permits ball to come to rest in one or both hands. While dribbling, player may take any number of steps between floor bounces.

Fade: To retreat to back court or defended basket.

Follow-In: A dash toward the basket to grab a rebound should one result.

Foul Line Notch: The point where the free throw lane meets the free throw circle.

Free Play: Slow deliberate offensive with much passing and faking, followed by a sudden concerted scoring effort should a defensive lapse occur. Also called "Eastern Style".

Give-And-Go: Offensive player passes to teammate then cuts for basket to either take a long return pass or draw the defense out of position.

Hacking: Striking an opponent's arms with the edge of the hand or with the hand. It is a personal foul.

Held Ball: A situation when two players on opposite teams have one or both hands on the ball; also, when a player withholds ball from play in his front court and makes no effort to put it in play, being too closely guarded. Necessitates a jump ball.

Hope Shot: A wild desperate shot at the basket, that has little chance of scoring.

Jacknife: The doubling action of the legs and body by a player taking a pass or a rebound from the backboard.

Kick: To strike the ball unintentionally with the knee or any part below the knee. Ball is then dead, and is awarded to opposing team from out of bounds.

Lay-Up: A one-hand bank shot taken after a cut or dribble into a point near the backboard.

Pick-Up Point: The part of the court where defensive men await their respective opponents and start a man-to-man-defense against them.

Restraining Circle: A circle of 6' radius in the center of the court, and concentric with the center circle.

Reverse Roll: Player fakes to go in front of a teammate, pivots, spins, and goes behind him.

Screening: An offensive player's attempt to protect a teammate's play by shutting off an opponent's approach without personal contact.

Set Shot: An unhurried long shot taken from a well-balanced position; usually a two-handed shot.

Shovel Pass: A short pass, one or two-handed, in which the ball, from a point near the floor, is "shoveled" up to a teammate.

Switching: A reversal of defensive positions. Players guarding certain opponents switch positions to guard other ones.

Throw-In: A method of putting the ball in play after it has gone out of bounds. It is thrown, rolled or bounced in by an opponent of the player who last touched it before it went out of bounds. The player has 5 seconds in which to put the ball in play.

Tip-In Shot: A shot in which a player tries to tip or deflect the ball, in the air and near the basket, into the basket.

Adapted From
THE DICTIONARY OF SPORTS by Parke Cummings.

A SUGGESTED BIBLIOGRAPHY

Books:

Allen, Forrest C., "Better Basketball," McGraw-Hill Book Co., Inc., 330 W. 42nd St., New York 18, N. Y.

Bee, Clair, "The Basketball Library." 1942. The Ronald Press Company, 15 East 26th Street, New York 10, N. Y.

Bee, Clair, and 75 noted coaches, "Winning Basketball Plays," 1950. The Ronald Press Company, 15 East 26th Street, New York 10, N. Y.

Bunn, "Basketball Methods." The MacMillan Co., 60 5th Ave., New York 11, N. Y.

Dean, Everett S., "Progressive Basketball," Prentice-Hall, Inc., 70 Fifth Ave., New York, N. Y.

Hobson, Howard A., "Basketball Illustrated." 1947. The Ronald Press Company, 15 East 26th Street, New York 10, N. Y.

Hobson, Howard, "Scientific Basketball." Prentice-Hall, Inc., 70 Fifth Ave., New York, N. Y.

Holman, Nat, "Holman on Basketball," 1951. Crown Publishers, New York City, New York.

Meissner, Wilhelmine E. and Meyers, Elizabeth Yeend, "Basketball For Girls," Revised, 1950. The Ronald Press Company, 15 East 26th Street, New York 10, N. Y.

Murphy, Charles, "Basketball." 1939. The Ronald Press Company, 15 East 26th Street, New York 10, N. Y.

Rupp, Adolph, "Rupp's Championship Basketball." Prentice-Hall, Inc., 70 Fifth Ave., New York, N. Y.

Schoor, Gene, "Giant Book of Sports". Doubleday & Co., Garden City, N. Y.

U. S. Naval Institute, "Basketball," 1943. A. S. Barnes Co., 11 East 36th Street, New York 16, N. Y.

Official Rules and Guide, National Basketball Committee. Produced and distributed by The National Collegiate Athletic Bureau, Box 757, Grand Central Station, New York 17, N. Y.